THE COUNTRY DIARY

BIRTHDAY BOOK

Edith Holden

CLAREMONT BOOKS

PENGUIN BOOKS
Published by the Penguin Group
Penguin Books Ltd, 27 Wrights Lane, London W8 5TZ, England
Penguin Books USA Inc., 375 Hudson Street, New York, New York 10014, USA
Penguin Books Australia Ltd, Ringwood, Victoria, Australia
Penguin Books Canada Ltd, 10 Alcorn Avenue, Toronto, Ontario, Canada M4V 3B2
Penguin Books (NZ) Ltd, 182–190 Wairau Road, Auckland 10, New Zealand

Penguin Books Ltd, Registered Offices, Harmondsworth, Middlesex, England

Designed by Ron Pickles

This edition Copyright © 1992 Michael Joseph Ltd

First Published in Great Britain 1987 by Webb & Bower Limited
in association with Michael Joseph Limited
First impression 1987
Second impression 1987
Third impression 1988
Fourth impression 1989
Fifth impression 1990
Sixth impression 1992

This edition published in 1996 by Claremont Books,
an imprint of Godfrey Cave Associates Limited,
42 Bloomsbury Street, London WC1B 3QJ, 1996

The illustrations in this book have been selected
from Edith Holden's *The Country Diary of an Edwardian Lady*,
published by Michael Joseph/Webb & Bower in 1977
Copyright © 1977 Richard Webb Ltd

We would like to thank Rowena Stott, Edith Holden's great-niece
and the owner of the original work, who has made this publication possible.

ISBN 1 85471 827 4

Printed in Great Britain

This perpetual Birthday Book is inspired by *The Country Diary of an Edwardian Lady*. For each day there is either a seasonal poem from *Country Diary*, a quotation from one of her favourite poets or a few lines by Edith Holden herself, describing the flora and fauna as she saw them in 1906, the year she wrote and illustrated her famous diary. Listed at the beginning of each month are birthdays of poets, artists and others who loved the countryside as Edith Holden did. Other books in this series are *The Country Diary Address Book* and *The Country Diary Year Book*.

January

Birthdays in January

January 1st	1767	Maria Edgeworth (novelist)
	1879	E. M. Forster (novelist)
January 4th	1878	Augustus John (painter)
January 5th	1789	Thomas Pringle (traveller and poet)
January 8th	1824	William Wilkie Collins (novelist)
January 17th	1820	Anne Brontë (poet and writer)
January 18th	1882	A. A. Milne (writer)
January 22nd	1788	George Gordon, Lord Byron (poet)
January 25th	1759	Robert Burns (poet)
January 27th	1832	Lewis Carroll (writer)
	1805	Samuel Palmer (painter)

JANUARY

1
Then came old January, wrapped well
In many weeds to keep the cold away
Yet did he quake and quiver like to quell
And blewe his nayles to warm them if he may

Faerie Queen, E Spenser.

2
I love the verse that, mild and bland,
Breathes of green fields and open sky.
I love the muse that in her hand
Bears flowers of native poesy

The Native Muse, John Clare

3
Daisies, those pearled Areturi of the earth,
The constellated flowers that never set.

Percy Bysshe Shelley

4
The poetry of earth is ceasing never;
On a lone winter evening when the frost
Has wrought a silence, from the stove there shrills
The Cricket's song, in warmth increasing ever

John Keats

5
This solitary Tree! a living thing
Produced too slowly ever to decay;
Of form and aspect too magnificent
To be destroyed.

Yew Trees, William Wordsworth

6   To him who in the love of Nature holds
    Communion with her visible forms, she speaks
    A various language
    William Cullen Bryant

7   Wee, modest, crimson-tipped flow'r
    Thou's met me in an evil hour;
    For I maun crush amang the stoure
                    Thy slender stem.
    To spare thee now is past my pow'r
                    Thou bonnie gem.
    To a mountain daisy. Robert Burns

8   The leaves which in the autumn of the year
    Fall auburn-tinted, leaving reft and bare
    Their parent trees, in many a sheltered lair
    Where winter waits and watches,
                            cold, austere,
    Old Year Leaves, Mackenzie Bell

9   But cease to move so near the Heavens, and cease
    To glide a sunbeam by the blasted Pine,
    To sit a star upon the sparkling spire;
    And come, for Love is of the valley, come.
    The Princess, Alfred, Lord Tennyson.

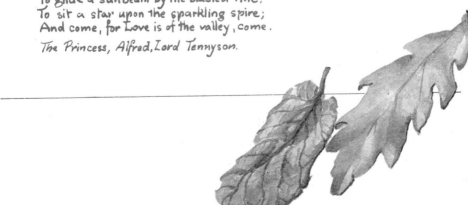

JANUARY

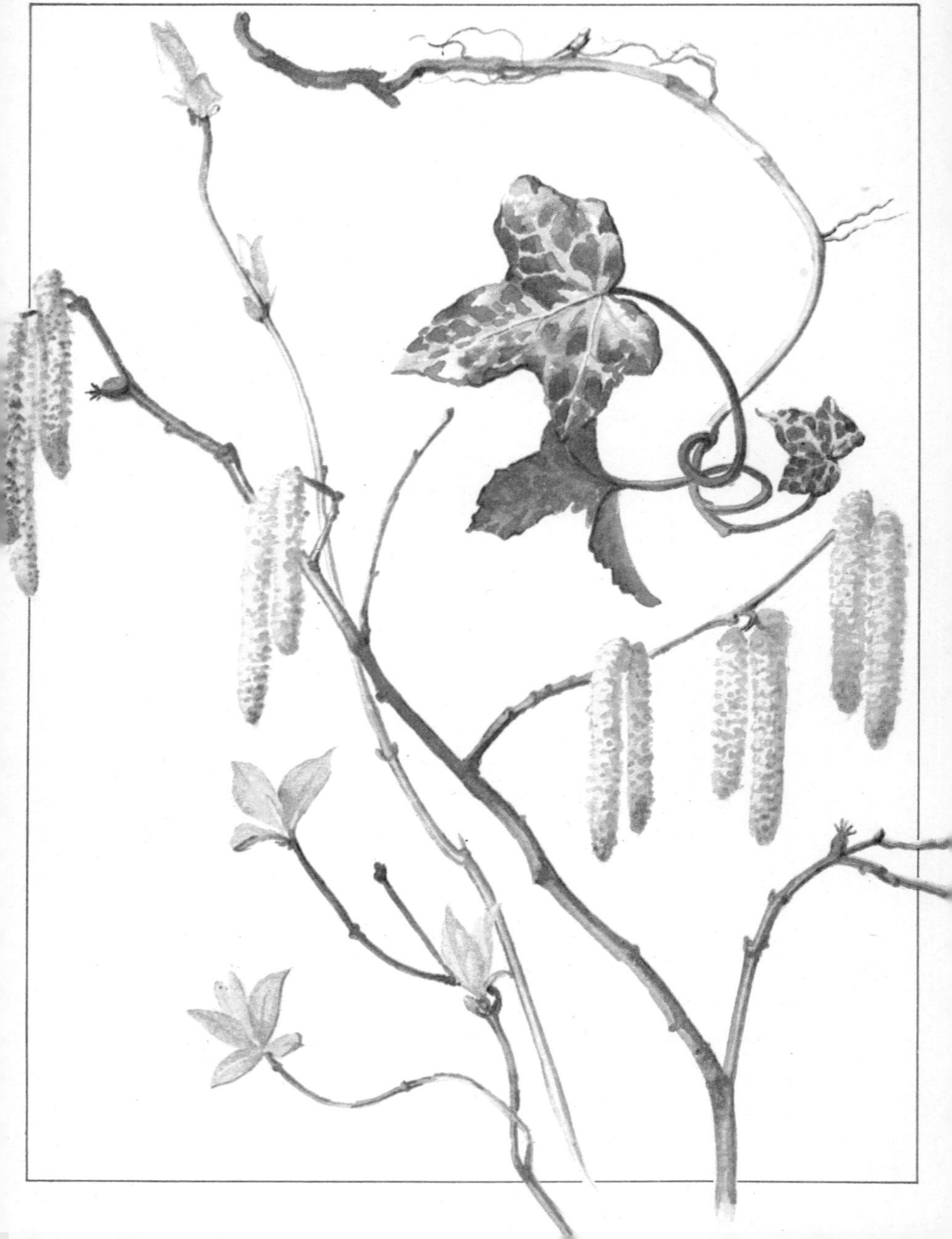

10 January - named from the Roman god Janus,
who is represented with two faces looking in
opposite directions, - as retrospective to the
past, and prospective to the coming year.
Edith Holden

11 Visited a small wood on the canal bank, to get
violet leaves. On moving away some of the dead
leaves lying beneath the trees, I discovered a
Wild Arum plant thrusting it's white sheath
up from the soil.
Edith Holden

12 Saw several Moorhens feeding on a
newly ploughed field, not far from a pond.
Edith Holden

13 Whither, midst falling dew,
While glow the heavens with the last steps of day,
Far, through their rosy depths, dost thou pursue
Thy solitary way?
To a Waterfowl, William Cullen Bryant

14 Above all flouris in the mede
Than I love most those flouris
White and rede;
Soche that men call daisies
In our towne
Chaucer

JANUARY

15

In winter when the dismal rain
Came down in slanting lines,
And Wind, that great old harper, smote
His thunder-harp of pines

Alexander Smith

16

Yew trees live to a great age, some in this
country being recorded as a thousand years of
age. It is supposed to have been planted by the
Druids in their sacred groves. In later days it
was planted in the church-yards as a symbol
of mourning

Edith Holden

17

The groundflame of the crocus breaks the mould,
Fair Spring slides hither o'er the Southern sea,
Wavers on her thin stem the snowdrop cold
That trembles not to kisses of the bee

Alfred, Lord Tennyson.

18

Today I saw a curious Oak-tree, growing in
a field near Elmdon Park. From a distance
it looked as if half of the tree were dead and
the other half covered with glossy green
leaves.

Edith Holden

19

The quiet lake, the balmy air,
The hill, the stream, the tower, the tree
Are they still such as once they were.
Or is the dreary change in me?

Sir Walter Scott

20 Thee Winter in the garland wears
That thinly decks his few grey hairs

To a Daisy . William Wordsworth.

21 Hark how the cheerefull birds do chaunt theyr laies
And carroll of loves praise.
The merry Larke hir mattins sings aloft,
The thrush replyes, the Mavis descant playes.

Edmund Spenser

22 Withering and keen the winter comes,
While Comfort flies to close-shut rooms,
And sees the snow in feathers pass
Winnowing by the window-glass

John Clare

Daisy
(Bellis perennis)

23

Went for a country walk. Every twig on
every tree and bush was outlined in silver
tracery against the sky.
Edith Holden

24

If January calends be summerly gay,
'Twill be winterly weather till the calends
of May

Anon.

25

Therefore all seasons shall be sweet to thee
Whether the summer clothe the general earth
With greenness, or the redbreast sit and sing
Betwixt the tufts of snow on the bare branch
Frost at Midnight. S.T. Coleridge

26

The last few weeks, our own and our
neighbours' garden have been haunted
by a very curious Robin
Edith Holden

27

Primroses, Polyanthus, Winter Aconite, Mazereon
and Snowdrops are all in flower in the garden.
Every mild morning now the birds are singing
and they continue more or less throughout
the day.
Edith Holden

28 Welcome, pale Primrose! starting up between
Dead matted leaves of ash and oak, that strew
The sunny lawn, the wood, and coppice through,
'Mid creeping moss and ivy's darker green

John Clare

29 Today I picked some Daisies in a field and saw
some Yew in blossom. The young Nettles are
shooting up and a number of herbaceous
plants are shewing new green leaves.

Edith Holden

30 Daisies, ye flowers of lowly birth
Embroiderers of the carpet earth
That gem the velvet sod

John Clare

31 I wonder if the sap is stirring yet,
If wintry birds are dreaming of a mate.
If frozen snowdrops feel as yet the sun
And crocus fires are kindling one by one

Christina Rossetti

February

Birthdays in February

February 3rd	1809 Felix Mendelssohn (composer)
February 6th	1564 Christopher Marlowe (writer)
February 7th	1812 Charles Dickens (novelist)
February 8th	1819 John Ruskin (writer)
February 10th	1670 William Congreve (poet and dramatist)
February 12th	1567 Thomas Campion (poet and musician)
	1809 Charles Darwin (naturalist)
	1815 Edward Forbes (naturalist)
	1828 George Meredith (poet)
February 23rd	1633 Samuel Pepys (diarist)
February 24th	1685 George Frederick Handel (composer)

FEBRUARY

1

One month is past, another is begun,
Since merry bells rang out the dying year,
And buds of rarest green began to peer,
As if impatient for a warmer sun

Feb 1st. 1842, Hartley Coleridge

2

If Candlemas Day be fair & bright
Winter will have another flight
But if Candlemas Day be clouds & rain
Winter is gone & will not come again!

Anon

3

It says in today's Chronicle that at Dover a
Blackbird's nest with two eggs has been found,
at Edenbridge a Hedge-sparrow's with four
eggs and at Elmstead, a robin's with five
eggs.

Edith Holden

4

O, Blackbird! sing me something well:
While all the neighbours shoot thee round,
I keep smooth plats of fruitful ground,
Where thou may'st warble, eat and dwell.

The Blackbird, Alfred, Lord Tennyson.

5

Mountain gorses, ever golden
Cankered not the whole year long!

E. B. Browning

6 Ah for pittie, wil rancke Winters rage,
These bitter blasts never ginne tasswage?
The kene cold blowes through my beaten hyde
All as I were through the body gryde.
The Shepheardes Calendar, February. Edmund Spenser

7 Picked some Dog's Mercury in flower; This
is the first to blossom of all the wild herbaceous
plants, Daisies and Groundsel excepted.
Edith Holden

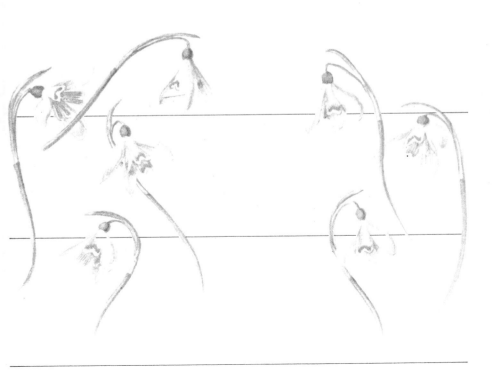

8
The snow-drop and then the violet,
Arose from the ground with warm rain wet,
And their breath was mixed with fresh odour, sent
From the turf, like the voice and the instrument.
Percy Bysshe Shelley

9
There were some terrible battles among the Tits
this morning. One tiny Blue-cap took possession
of the cocoa-nut sitting down in the middle of
it and bidding defiance to all the others. It
was very funny to see
Edith Holden

10
In February, if thou hearest thunder
Thou shalt see a summer wonder
Anon

11
That strain again; it had a dying fall:
O, it came o'er my ear like the sweet south
That breathes upon a bank of Violets
Stealing and giving odour
William Shakespeare

12
I visited the violet wood again today, the
Lords and Ladies are quite up above the
ground now; and the Violets roots are
sending up little green trumpets of new
leaves.
Edith Holden

13 A violet by a mossy stone
Half- hidden from the eye!
Fair as a star, when only one
Is shining in the sky
William Wordsworth

14 And now all Nature seem'd in love;
The lusty sap began to move;
New juice did stir th'embracing vines;
And birds had drawn their Valentines
Sir Henry Wotton

15 I saw two little Shrew-Mice in different
places on the bank, who darted quickly
into their holes directly they saw me.
Edith Holden

16 Heard the Lark singing for the first
time this year
Edith Holden

17 The Erd-Shrew or Shrew-Mouse, inhabits
subterranean tunnels which it excavates in
the soil. It feeds upon insects and worms;
and its long, flexible nose is a great aid
to it in it's search after food.
Edith Holden

18 Wee, sleekit, cow'rin, timrous beastie,
O what a panic's i' thy breastie!
Thou needna start awa' sae hasty
            Wi' bickering brattle!
I wad be laith to rin and chase thee
             Wi' murd'ring prattle!
To a Mouse, Robert Burns

19 The blackbird's note comes mellower from the dale;
And sweeter from the sky the gladsome lark
Warbles his heaven-tuned song; the lulling brook
Murmurs more gently down the deep-worn glen

Reverend James Grahame

20 Henceforth I shall know
That Nature ne'er deserts the wise and pure;
No plot so narrow, be but Nature there,

Samuel Taylor Coleridge

21

Willows whiten, aspens quiver,
Little breezes dusk and shiver
Through the wave that runs for ever
By the island in the river
The Lady of Shalott, Alfred, Lord Tennyson

22

Then came old February, sitting
In an old wagon, for he could not ride,
Drawn of two fishes for the season fitting,
Which through the flood before did softly slide
Edmund Spenser

23

Where luscious dewdrops lurk,
I with fifty went to work,
Catching delicious wine, that wets
The warm blue heart of violets
William Allingham

24

The farmer (at Packwood Hall) brought out a
little lamb to show me, one of a family of
three born that morning. I held it in my
arms and it seemed quite fearless – poking
it's little black head up into my face
Edith Holden

25

The green earth echoed to the feet
Of lambs that bounded through the glade,
From shade to sunshine, and as fleet
From sunshine back to shade
William Wordsworth

26   Now the North wind ceases;
The warm South-west awakes,
The heavens are out in fleeces
And earth's green banner shakes

George Meredith

27   Come when the rains
Have glazed the snow and clothed the trees with ice,
While slant sun of February pour
Into the bowers a flood of light.

William Cullen Bryant

28   Ash Wednesday.
We have had more winter weather this
February than any other month this winter.

Edith Holden.

29   Day!
Faster and more fast,
O'er night's brim, day boils at last;
Boils, pure gold, o'er the cloud-cup's brim
Where spurting and supprest it lay.

Robert Browning

March

Birthdays in March

March 6th	1806	Elizabeth Barrett Browning (poet)
March 7th	1802	Sir Edwin Henry Landseer (painter)
March 8th	1763	William Cobbett (writer)
	1859	Kenneth Grahame (writer)
March 17th	1846	Kate Greenaway (illustrator)
March 22nd	1599	Anthony Van Dyke (painter)
March 24th	1834	William Morris (writer)
March 26th	1859	A.E Houseman (scholar and poet)
March 31st	1611	Andrew Marvell (poet)

MARCH

1 March has come in like a lamb with a
warm wind and rain from the south-west
Edith Holden

2 So many misties in March
So many frosties in May
Anon

3 What did Spring-time whisper?
O ye rivulets,
Waking from your trance so sad,
Pleased to welcome fisher-lad
With his little nets
Norman Gale

4 Went for a long walk. Found the Colt's-foot
and Procumbent Field Speedwell in flower
Edith Holden

5 It is the first mild day of March:
Each minute sweeter than before,
The redbreast sings from the tall larch
That stands beside our door
William Wordsworth

6   Tonight a Toad was discovered jumping about
in the hall; it must have come in through
the garden door which has been standing
open all day.

     Edith Holden

7   Bring hether the Pincke and purple Cullambine,
       With Gelliflowres;
Bring Coronations, and Sops in wine,
       Worne of Paramoures.
Strowe me the ground with Daffadowndillies
Edmund Spenser

8   When daffodils begin to peer,
With heigh, the doxy o'er the dale,
Why then comes in the sweet o' the year,
For the red blood reigns in the water pale.

     Shakespeare

MARCH

9 The stormy March is come at last
   With wind, and cloud, and changing skies;
   I hear the rushing of the blast
   That through the snowy valley flies.

   William Cullen Bryant

10 A beautiful jay in all the glory of his spring
   plumage flew screaming across the lane into
   a spinney of larch trees opposite. He seemed
   to resent the intrusion of a human being
   in such an unfrequented spot.

   Edith Holden

11 Through primrose tufts in that green bower
The periwinkle trailed its wreathes
And tis my faith that every flower
Enjoys the air it breathes.

Lines written in early Spring, by William Wordsworth

12 After a wet, windy day, we wake this morning
to a regular snow storm, the air was full of
whirling flakes, but in the midst of it all
I heard a Sky-lark singing.

Edith Holden

13 The cold has almost silenced the birds this
morning. Numbers of them came onto the
lawn to be fed, the Starlings and cock
Chaffinches look specially gay just now in
their spring coats.

Edith Holden

14 In the afternoon I went to the violet-wood,
and to my surprise I found a number of
flowing, purple blossoms in the sheltered
glades of the wood.

Edith Holden

15 Violets dim yet sweeter than the lids of
Juno's eyes or Cytherea's breathe

Winter's Tale, William Shakespeare

16 Daffy-down-dilly is come up to town,
In her yellow petticoat and her green gown.

Anon

17 Daffodils that come before the swallow dares,
And take the winds of March with beauty.

William Shakespeare

18 And the Spring arose on the garden fair,
Like the Spirit of Love felt everywhere;
And each flower and herb on Earth's dark breast
Rose from the dreams of its wintry rest.

Percy Bysshe Shelley

19 Then the thrushes sang
And shook my pulses and the elm's new leaves.

Elizabeth Barrett Browning

20 Found two Thrush's nests, both in holly bushes;
one nest was empty, the bird was sitting on the
other; she looked at me with such brave, bright
eyes, I could not disturb her, much as I would
have liked a peep at her speckled eggs.

Edith Holden

21 How sweet the hedge that hides a cunning nest,
And curtains off a patient bright-eyed thrush,
With five small worlds beneath her mottled breast!
A Creed, Norman Gale

22 Gloomy winters' now awa'
Soft the westlin breezes blaw,
'Mong the birks o' Stanley shaw,
The mavis sings fu'cheerie, O.
R. Tannahill

23 In days when daisies deck the sod
And blackbirds whistle dear.
Wi' honest joy our hearts will bound
To greet the coming year.
Robert Burns

24 Ye violets that first appear
By your pure purple mantles known.
Sir Henry Wotton

MARCH

25
That's the wise thrush, he sings his song twice over.
Lest you should think he never could recapture
That first, fine, careless rapture.
Robert Browning

26
As violets recluse and sweet,
Cheerful as daisies unaccounted rare;
Still sunward gazing from a lowly seat,
Still sweetening wintry air.
Christina Rossetti

27
And hark! how blithe the Throstle sings,
He, too, is no mean preacher;
Come forth into the light of things
Let Nature be your teacher.
William Wordsworth

28
Gathered some of the young crimson catkins
of the Black Poplar. The last few days have
been very cold and dry, with keen north wind,
and any quantity of March dust in
evidence.
Edith Holden

29
The snowdrop and primrose
Our woodlands adorn
And violets bathe mid the weet
O' the morn
Robert Burns

30 There is a Flower, the lesser Celandine,
That shrinks, like many more, from cold and rain;
And, the first moment that the sun may shine,
Bright as the sun himself, 'tis out again!

The Small Celandine, William Wordsworth

31 Everywhere the celandine made the
ditches bright, and the strawberry-
leaved cinque-foil spangled the banks.

Edith Holden

Sweet Violet (Viola odorata)

APRIL

Birthdays in April

April 3rd	1593	George Herbert (poet)
April 5th	1837	Algernon Charles Swinburne (poet)
April 7th	1770	William Wordsworth (poet)
April 8th	1783	John C. Loudon (landscape gardener)
April 10th	1778	William Hazlitt (writer)
April 11th	1772	Christopher Smart (poet)
April 15th	1843	Henry James (writer)
April 16th	1871	James Millington Synge (dramatist and poet)
April 17th	1622	Henry Vaughan (poet)
April 21st	1816	Charlotte Brontë (novelist)
April 22nd	1707	Henry Fielding (dramatist and novelist)
April 23rd	1564	William Shakespeare (playwright and poet)
	1775	Joseph Mallord William Turner (painter)
April 24th	1815	Anthony Trollope (novelist)
April 25th	1769	Sir Mark Isambard Brunel (engineer)
	1873	Walter de la Mare (poet)
April 26th	1785	John James Audubon (painter)
April 27th	1759	Mary Wollstonecraft (writer)

1   I went to a little spinney to see a large bush of
the Great Round-leaved Willow, which is a perfect
picture just now; covered all over with great
golden catkins, that light up the copse like
hundreds of little fairy lamps.
Edith Holden

2   Oh; how this spring of love resembleth
The uncertain glory of an April day!
Which now shows all the beauty of the sun
And by and bye a cloud takes all away

Two Gentlemen of Verona, William Shakespeare

3   Come forth, ye blossoms! - over hill and lea,
A breathe of sweetness wantons with the sea;
And mid the smiles and tears of tender Spring,
On dripping boughs I heard the throstle sing.

A Song of Salutation, E.M. Holden

4   Third day of bright sunshine. I found
another field of wild Daffodils today. The sun
has brought out the green leaf-buds on the
trees and hedges very rapidly.

Edith Holden

5
Oh, to be in England now that April's there
And whoever wakes in England sees, some morning, unaware,
That the lowest boughs and the brushwood sheaf
Round the elm tree bole are in tiny leaf

Robert Browning

6
My earliest love of flowers, how good
To lay my sunburnt face,
In grass so lush,
It shames the name of green

Alfred Hayes

7
The Tadpoles have come out of their balls of
jelly and career madly about the aquarium
wagging their little black tails. A Gudgeon
which had been put into the aquarium has made
a meal of a good many of them.

Edith Holden

8   And wind-flowers and violets
    Which yet join not scent to hue
    Crown the pale year weak and new
    Shelley

9   The low-lying fertile lands round the Avon in
    Worcestershire were golden with Marsh
    Marigolds, and as we went through Glouce-
    stershire the banks were starred with
    Primroses and I saw a good many Cowslips.
    Edith Holden

10 Now blooms the lily on the bank
    The primrose down the brae;
    The hawthorn's budding in the glen
    And milk-white is the slae!
    Robert Burns

11 Up on the moor the world seemed to be
    made up of sky and gorse, – such acres of
    fragrant, golden blossom under a sky of
    cloudless blue.
    Edith Holden

12 It was an April morning: fresh and clear
    The Rivulet, delighting in its strength,
    Ran with a young man's speed
    William Wordsworth

APRIL

13 We saw a heron rise through the trees on
the opposite slope and sail away over the
wood, the pink and grey tints of his legs and
plumage, showing up very distinctly
against the brown background of bare trees.
Edith Holden

14 Saw the first Swallow and a yellow
Brimstone Butterfly
Edith Holden

15 Easter Sunday. Another brilliant day. Saw
a pair of House Martins, watched some
Trout in the Leet and found a Chaffinch's
nest nearly finished in a young Hawthorn.
Edith Holden

16 Long as there's a sun that sets
Primroses will have their glory
Long as there are violets
They will have a place in story
William Wordsworth

17 The wall-banks that divide the fields here
and run along the lanes are beginning to
be enamelled with little flowers and
ferns, and on the broad tops, crowned with low
hedges, the Blue-Bells are coming up very thickly.
Edith Holden

18 Tis the merry nightingale
    That crowds and hurries and precipitates,
    With fast, thick warble, his delicious notes
    Samuel Taylor Coleridge

19 Going over Yannaden Down we saw a young
    hare lying in it's form among the gorse
    bushes. It lay quite still till we had all
    but trodden on it
    Edith Holden

20 Next came fresh April, full of lustyhed,
    And wanton as a kid whose horne new buds;
    Upon a bull he rode, the same which led
    Europa floating through th'Argolick fluds
    Edmund Spenser

21 Are not our lowing heifers sleeker than
Night swollen mushrooms? Are not our wide plains
Speckled with countless fleeces? Have not rains
Green'd over April's lap

John Keats

22 The ground was carpeted with Anemones and
Blue-bells and here and there Primroses;
and the tall, handsome plants of the Wood
Spurge were very conspicuous with their
red stalks and pale green flowers

Edith Holden

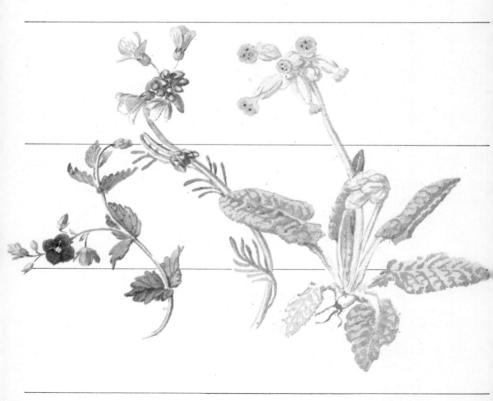

23   A Hawk suddenly sailed into the sea of gold above the setting sun and remained stationary, poised on quivering wing for quite a long time, then it suddenly dived down into the purple shadows of the plantation
                     just below

Edith Holden

24   Cuckoo! Cuckoo! he sings again,
      his notes are void of art.
But simplest strains do soonest sound
      the deep founts of the heart.

William Motherwell

25   Found two more Chaffinch's nests today, and a Hedge Sparrow's nests with four eggs. The Willow Wren has put in his appearance here the last day or two.

Edith Holden

26 I come, I come! ye have called me long,
I come o'er the mountains with light and song!
Ye may trace my steps o'er the wakening earth,
By the winds that tell of the violets' birth

Mrs Felicia Dorothea Hemans

27 Now fades the last long streak of snow,
Now burgeons every maze of quick
About the flowering squares, and thick
By ashen roots the violets blow

Alfred, Lord Tennyson

28 Go out, children, from the mine and from the city;
Sing out, children, as the little thrushes do;
Pluck your handfuls of the meadow-cowslips pretty,
Laugh aloud to let your fingers let them through!

The Cry of the Children. Elizabeth Barrett Browning

29 When I looked out this morning the
landscape was all white; the distant
tors veiled in a mist of driving sleet.

Edith Holden

30 When daisies red and violets blue
And ladies' Smocks' all silver white
And cuckoo-birds of yellow hue
Do paint the meadows with delight.

William Snakespeare

White Dead Nettle *(lamium album)*

Red Dead Nettle
(lamium purpureum)

Wood Crowfoot
(Ranunculous auricornus)

Common Avens
(Geum urbinus)

MAY

Birthdays in May

May 2nd	1779	John Galt (writer)
	1859	Jerome K. Jerome (writer)
May 7th	1812	Robert Browning (poet)
May 9th	1860	J. M. Barrie (writer)
May 12th	1812	Edward Lear (artist and writer)
	1828	Dante Gabriel Rossetti (painter and poet)
May 13th	1842	Sir Arthur Sullivan (composer)
May 16th	1782	John Sell Cotman (painter)
May 21st	1688	Alexander Pope (poet)
May 23rd	1799	Thomas Hood (poet and writer)
May 29th	1874	G. K. Chesterton (writer)

MAY

1

The primroses are still thick on the banks,
the hedges are green, many of the Apple
orchards in blossom; and the Oaks
showing the first signs of golden bronze
foliage.
Edith Holden

2

Tomorrow'll be the happiest time of all the
                                  glad New Year;
Of all the glad New Year, mother, the maddest,
                                  merriest day;
For I'm to be Queen o' the May, mother,
                       I'm to be Queen o' the May.

The May Queen, Alfred, Lord Tennyson

3

Gathered some wild Pear.Blossom and
the first Cow-slips I have picked this year.
Saw two hen Blackbirds sitting on their
nests — one in a hollow tree
Edith Holden

4

Then came faire May, the fairest mayde on grounde;
Deckt all with dainties of her seasons pryde,
And trowing flowers out of her lap arounde;
Upon two Bretheren's shoulders she did ride
Edmund Spenser

5

I saw a pair of white-throats today down
Widney Lane, they were evidently rivals
and were chasing each other through
the bushes, singing loudly all the time.

Edith Holden

White-throat and nest.

6 Thou, Linnet in thy green array,
   Presiding Spirit here to-day
   Dost lead the revels of the May;
   And this is thy dominion.
   William Wordsworth

7 The Crab-apple trees and bushes are
   looking very beautiful now, covered
   with pink blossom and crimson buds.
   Edith Holden

8 I dared to rest, or wander, in a rest
   Made sweeter by the step upon the grass,
   And view the ground's most gentle
                              dimplement
   (As if God's finger touched, but did not press
   In making England).
   Aurora Leigh, Elizabeth Barrett Browning

Red Campion
(Lychnis diurna)
Wild Hyacinth
(agraphis nutans)

Wild Beaked Parsley
(Anthriscus sylvestris)

9   I brought home a big bunch of Blue-bells,
    Red Campion and Wild-Beaked Parsley,
    the latter is showing it's white umbrels
    of blossom in every hedgerow.
    Edith Holden

10 O velvet bee, your're a dusty fellow;
    You've powdered your legs with gold!
    O brave marshmary buds, rich and yellow;
    Give me your money to hold!
    Jean Ingelow

11 Full flowered, and visible on every steep,
    Along the copses runs in veins of gold.
    William Wordsworth

12 I gathered Hawthorn Blossom from the
    hedges, and saw fields yellow with
    Buttercups and banks of Blue Speedwell.
    Edith Holden

13 Shaded hyacinth, alway
    Sapphire queen of the mid-May;
    And every leaf, and every flower
    Pearlèd with the self-same shower.
    John Keats

MAY

14 The ground was covered with Wild Arums, all
in flower, – their pale green spathes gleaming
out very conspicuously against the red
earthen banks where the rabbits burrow.
Edith Holden

15 Above in the wind was the swallow,
Chasing itself at its own wild will,
And far thro' the marish green and still
The tangled water-courses slept,
Shot over with purple, and green, and yellow
Alfred, Lord Tennyson.

16 This afternoon I went to gather Cuckoo-
pints for my drawing-class. Going through
the wood I picked up a Thrush's egg, lying
on the ground under the trees. Some of the
Horse Chestnut trees are a mass of white
blossom
Edith Holden

17 Hedgerows all alive
With birds and gnats and large white butterflies
Which look as if the Mayflower had caught life
And palpated forth upon the wind.
Elizabeth Barrett Browning

18 Come. Queen of Months in company
With all thy merry minstrelsy;
The restless cuckoo, absent long,
And twittering swallows' chimney-song
John Clare

19 I also gathered the Yellow Weasel Snout, Lady's
Mantle, Field Scorpion Grass and the Garlic,
the latter just breaking through it's green
sheathe. The hedgerows are haunted by
young fledgelings.
Edith Holden

20 Among the many buds proclaiming May
Decking the fields in holiday array,
Striving who shall surpass in braverie;
Marke the faire flowering of the hawthorne tree

Chaucer

21 Fast fading violets cover'd up in leaves;
And mid-May's eldest child,
The coming musk-rose, full of dewy wine,
The murmurous haunt of flies on summer eves.

John Keats

Flower
of the Sycamore
or Plane-tree
(Acer pseudo-platanus)

MAY

22 And in the warm hedge grew lush eglantine,
Green cowbind and the moonlight-coloured may,
And cherry-blossoms and white cups, whose wine
Was the bright dew, yet drained not by the day

Percy Bysshe Shelley

23 Ye that pipe and ye that play
Ye that through your hearts today
Feel the gladness of the May

Ode: William Wordsworth

24 For May wol have no slogardie a-night,
The seson priketh every gentil herte,
And maketh him out of his slepe to sterte

The Knightes Tale, Geoffrey Chaucer

25 An angel mid the woods of May
Embroidered it with radiance gay -
That gossamer with gold bedight -
Those fires of God - those gems of light.

From the Welsh of Dafydd ap Gwilym

26 Walking through the fields today I gathered
the pretty little Yellow Heartsease;
growing among the grass and clover.

Edith Holden

27 All Nature seems at work. Slugs have their lair -
The bees are stirring - birds are on the wing —
And Winter, slumbering in the open air,
Wears on his smiling face a dream of Spring!

Samuel Taylor Coleridge

28 Ye flowery banks o' bonie Doon,
How can ye blume sae fair?
How can ye chant, ye little birds,
And I sae fu' o' care?

Robert Burns

29 Saw some Dog Daisies in flower on the
railway bank. My sister brought home
some beautiful White Meadow Saxifrage she
had picked in some fields near Hatton. Common
Earth Nut, Fumitory and Black Meddick in flower.

Edith Holden

30 More pleasant far to me the broom
That blows sae fair on Cowden Knowes
For sure sae sweet, sae soft a bloom
Elsewhere there never grows.

Scotch song

31 No daintie flowre or herbe that growes on grownd,
No arborett with painted blossoms drest
And smelling sweete, but there it might be fownd
To bud out faire, and throwe her sweete
                              smels al arownd

Edmund Sponser

JUNE

Birthdays in June

June 1st	1879	John Masefield (poet)
June 2nd	1840	Thomas Hardy (novelist)
June 7th	1825	R. D. Blackmore (novelist)
June 11th	1572	Ben Jonson (writer)
	1776	John Constable (painter)
June 12th	1819	Charles Kingsley (writer)
June 13th	1752	Fanny Burney (writer)
	1865	William Butler Yeats (writer and poet)
June 14th	1726	Thomas Pennant (traveller and naturalist)
June 15th	1605	Thomas Randolph (poet and dramatist)
June 22nd	1876	Gwen John (painter)
June 30th	1685	John Gay (writer)

JUNE

1
And after her came jolly June, array'd
All in green leaves, as he a player were;
Yet in his time he wrought as well as play'd,
That by his plough-yrons mote right well appeare

Edmund Spenser

2
Many of the meadows are golden with
Buttercups, and some of the fields are
showing quite red, where the Sorrel is
coming into flower.

Edith Holden

3
Now summer is in flower, and Nature's hum
Is never silent round her bounteous bloom,
Insects, as small as dust, have never done
With glitt'ring dance, and reeling in the sun.

John Clare

4
Whit-Monday. Another summer day.
Gathered the Greater Celandine and saw
the Brooklime and Yellow Rattle in
flower

Edith Holden

5
I know a bank whereon the Wild-Thyme blows,
Where Oxlips & the nodding Violet grows.
Quite overcanopied with lush Woodbine
With sweet Musk-roses & with Eglantine.

William Shakespeare

6   The common was covered with short grass
    and furze bushes and smelt deliciously of
    Thyme, though we found none quite in
    flower.
    Edith Holden

7   A cloudless sky; a world of heather,
    Purple of foxglove; yellow of broom;
    We two among it, wading together;
    Shaking out honey, treading perfume

    Jean Ingelow

Wild Guelder Rose
(Viburnum opulus)

JUNE

8   I saw an owl tonight, flying across the
gardens at the back of the St. Bernard's
Road. This is the first one I have seen
at Olton
Edith Holden

9   G brought in some blossoms of the
dusky cranesbill today. She picked them
on the bank of a lane near Sheldon. In
all probability the seed of the plant had
been carried there from some garden.
Edith Holden

10   Why will your mind for ever go
To meads in sunny Greece?
Our songsbirds have as fine a flow,
Our sheep as fair a fleece;
Norman Gale

11   Three beauteous springs to yellow autumn turn'd
In process of the seasons have I seen,
Three April perfumes in three hot Junes burn'd,
Since first I saw you fresh, which yet are green.
William Shakespeare

12   Silver-weed, Wood Sanicle, Rough Hawk-Bit,
Small Hairy Willow-Herb and Comfrey in
blossom. The Wild Service-tree has been
in flower for some weeks.
Edith Holden

Fox-glove (*Digitalis purpurea*)
Trailing Rose (*Rosa arvensis*)

JUNE

13 I gathered some Figwort and Celery-leaved
Crowfoot this afternoon in a ditch in
Elmdon Park. Also found the Bittersweet,
Black Bryony and Creeping Cinquefoil in
flower.
Edith Holden

14 Wild Guelder Rose, Elderberry and Wild
Angelica in blossom.
Edith Holden

15 It is very pretty to see the House Martins
sitting on the roadway, collecting mud
for their nests. Their short feathered
legs look as if they had little white socks
on.
Edith Holden

16 Saw the first Wild Rose in bloom, – a fine
pink one, on the top of a high hedge;
also Blackberry in blossom. The Roses
and Honeysuckle are full of bud
Edith Holden

17 For the Rose, ho, the Rose! is the eye of the flowers
Is the blush of the meadows that feel themselves fair,
Is the lightning of beauty that strikes thro' the bowers,
On pale lovers who sit in the glow unaware.
E.B.B. trans from Sappho

Creeping Cinquefoil
(*Potentilla reptans*)

18 In puffs of balm the night-air blows
The perfume which the day fore-goes.
And on the pure horizon far,
See, pulsing with the first-born star

The Liquid sky, Matthew Arnold

19 This morn is merry June, I trow,
The rose is budding fain;
But she shall bloom in winter snow
Ere we two meet again.

Sir Walter Scott

20 The pleached bower
Where honeysuckles, ripened by the sun,
Forbid the sun to enter

Much Ado ~ Shakespeare

21 Stay, ruby-breasted warbler, stay,
And let me see thy sparkling eye.
Oh brush not yet the pearl-strung spray
Nor bow thy pretty head to fly.

John Keats

JUNE

22 All June I bound the rose in sheaves
Now, rose by rose, I strip the leaves
And strew them where Pauline may pass.
She will not turn aside? Alas!
Robert Browning

23 At the edge of the stream I found the large
blue water forget-me-not. While I was
stooping to gether some, a beautiful
demoiselle dragonfly came skimming across
the water and lighted on a bunch of rushes.
Edith Holden

24 The Cuckoo is beginning to change his
tune, a little later he will be saying
'cuc-cuckoo' instead of 'cuckoo'.
Edith Holden

25 Everywhere the lanes were fragrant with
wild roses, and honeysuckle, and the breeze
came to us over the hedges laden with
the perfume of the clover-fields and
grass meadows.
Edith Holden

26 The cuckoo is a fine bird,
She whistles as she flies
And as she whistles, Cuckoo!
The bluer grow the skies.
Anon

27 All twinkling with the dewdrop's sheen
The briar-rose falls in streamer's green.

Sir Walter Scott

28 My love is like a red, red rose
That's newly sprung in June:
My love is like the melody
That's sweetly played in tune.

Robert Burns

29 Where the bee sucks, there suck I:
In a cowslip's bell I lie;
There I couch when owls do cry,
On a bat's back I do fly

William Shakespeare

30 Scarlet Poppy, Sow Thistle, Plume
Thistle and Wild Migonette in flower.

Edith Holden

Dog Roses (*Rosa canina*)

JULY

Birthdays in July

July 1st	1804	George Sand (novelist)
July 8th	1823	Sir Henry Raeburn (painter)
July 11th	1834	James Whistler (painter)
July 16th	1723	Sir Joshua Reynolds (painter)
July 18th	1720	Gilbert White (naturalist)
	1811	William Makepeace Thackeray (writer)
July 23rd	1823	Coventry Patmore (poet)
July 26th	1856	George Bernard Shaw (writer)
July 27th	1777	Thomas Campbell (poet)
July 28th	1844	Gerard Manley Hopkins (poet)
July 30th	1818	Emily Brontë (writer)

JULY

1
Then came hot July, boyling like to fire,
That all his garments he had cast away,
Upon a Lyon raging yet with ire
He boldly 'rode , and made him to obaye

Edmund Spenser

2
July, the month of summer's prime,
Again resumes his busy time ;
Scythes tinkle in each grassy dell ;
And meadows , they are mad with noise

John Clare

3
Yellow with birdfoot-trefoil are the grass glades ;
Yellow with cinquefoil of the dew-gray leaf ;
Yellow with stone crop ; the moss-mounds are yellow

Love in the Valley, George Meredith

4
A swarm of bees in May is worth a load of hay,
A swarm of bees in June is worth a silver spoon,
A swarm of bees in July is not worth a fly.

Anon

5
The clearest echoes of the hills,
The softest notes of falling rills ,
The melodies of birds and bees,
The murmuring of the summer seas

Percy Bysshe Shelley

Red Admiral
Butterfly (Vanessa Atalanta)

6   Miss F. gave me some bee orchids this
    afternoon which she had gathered
    growing wild in Berkshire.
    Edith Holden

7   The marsh at Widney is quite blue in
    some places with the large Water
    For-get-me-not and the ditches were
    lined with masses of creamy Meadow
    Sweet.
    Edith Holden

8   Now folds the lily all her sweetness up,
    And slips into the bosom of the lake:
    So fold thyself, my dearest, thou, and slip
    Into my bosom and be lost in me.

    Alfred, Lord Tennyson

9   Far, far around shall those dark-cluster'd trees
    Fledge the wild-ridged mountains steep by steep;
    And there by zephyrs, streams, and birds, and bees,
    The moss-lain Dryads shall be lull'd to sleep

    John Keats

10 Caverns there were within my mind, which sun
Could never penetrate, yet did there not
Want store of leafy arbours where the light
Might enter in at will.
William Wordsworth

11 ... there were numbers of flowers growing
among the grasses; quantities of the deep,
crimson heads of Great Burnet, Dog Daisies,
Self-heal, Yellow Rattle, Knapweed, Spotted
Orchis and Yellow and purple Vetches.
Edith Holden

12 And I serve the fairy queen,
To dew her orbs upon the green:
The cowslips tall her pensioners be;
In their gold coats spots you see
Fairy Song, William Shakespeare

13 And there were gardens bright with sinuous rills
Where blossomed many an incense-bearing tree;
And here were forest ancient as the hills,
Enfolding sunny spots of greenery.
Kubla Khan, Samuel Taylor Coleridge

14 Saw the following flowers in bloom since I
passed through the lanes a week ago,—
Field Knautia, Small Scabious, Nipplewort,
Water Dropwort, Corn Sow Thistle, Creeping
Plume Thistle and Ivy-leaved Lettuce
Edith Holden

Small Tortoiseshell
(Vanessa Urticæ)

Meadow Sweet
or
Queen of the Meadow
(Spiræa salicifolia)

Small Upright St John's Wort
(Hypericum pulchrum)

Stinging Nettle
(Urtica Dioica)

15 Saw a Blackbird sitting on it's nest
today, in the top of a high Hawthorn
hedge
Edith Holden

16 The lovely laughter of the wind-swayed wheat,
The easy slope of yonder pastoral hill,
The sedgy brook where by the red kine meet,
And wade, and drink their fill.
Jean Ingelow

17 Yet Brignall banks are fresh and fair,
And Greta woods are green,
And you may gather garlands there
Would grace a summer-queen
Sir Walter Scott

18 Now all the tree-tops lay asleep
Like green waves on the sea,
As still as in the silent deep
The ocean-woods may be.
    Percy Bysshe Shelley

19 And forth on floating gauze, no jewelled queen,
So rich, the green-eyed dragon-flies would break
And hover on the flowers — aerial things;
With little rainbows flickering on their wings
    Jean Ingelow

20 The summer's flower is to the summer sweet;
Though to itself it only live and die;
But if that flower with base infection meet,
The basest weed outbraves his dignity
    William Shakespeare

21 This is a beautiful bit of country, - low-
lying meadows with sedgy streams,
meandering through them, lined with
beds of water-flowers and rushes.
    Edith Holden

22 These hedge-rows, hardly hedge-rows, little lines
Of sportive wood run wild; these pastoral farms,
Green to the very door; and wreaths of smoke
Sent up, in silence, from among the trees!
    William Wordsworth

JULY

23 Toadflax, ragweed and tansy in bloom

   Edith Holden

24 Full many a glorious morning have I seen,
   Flatter the mountain tops with sovereign eye,
   Kissing with golden face the meadows green;
   Gilding pale streams with heavenly alchemy

   William Shakespeare

25 Soon will the high Midsummer pomps come on,
   Soon will the musk carnations break and swell,
   Soon shall we have gold-dusted snapdragon,
   Sweet-William with his homely cottage-smell.

   Matthew Arnold

26 Sweeter thy voice, but every sound is sweet;
   Myriads of rivulets hurrying thro' the lawn,
   The moan of doves in immemorial elms,
   And murmuring of innumerable bees.

   Alfred, Lord Tennyson

27 The trees are here all green again,
   Here bees the flower still kiss,
   But flowers and trees seemed sweeter then:
   My early home was this.

   John Clare

28

Full half an hour, to-day, I tried my lot
With various flowers, and every one still said,
'She loves me – loves me not.'
And if this meant a vision long since fled

Percy Bysshe Shelley

29

Mother of the dews, dark eye-lashed twilight,
Low-lidded twilight, o'er the valley's brim,
Rounding on thy breast sings the dew-delighted skylark,
Clear as though the dewdrops had their voice in him.

George Meredith

30

Yet let us think upon the vernal showers
That gladden the green earth, and we shall find
A pleasure in the dimness of the stars.
And hark! the Nightingale begins its song.

The Nightingale, Samuel Taylor Coleridge

31

Happy is England! I could be content
To see no other verdure than it's own;
To feel no other breezes than are blown
Through its tall woods with high romances blent.

John Keats

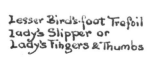

Lesser Bird's-foot Trefoil
lady's Slipper or
Lady's Fingers & Thumbs

AUGUST

Birthdays in August

August 1st	1743	Richard Savage (poet)
August 4th	1792	Percy Bysshe Shelley (poet)
August 6th	1809	Alfred Lord Tennyson (poet)
August 9th	1593	Isaak Walton (The Compleat Angler)
	1631	John Dryden (poet)
August 12th	1774	Robert Southey (poet)
August 15th	1771	Sir Walter Scott (poet and novelist)
August 21st	1872	Aubrey Vincent Beardsley (illustrator)
August 24th	1591	Robert Herrick (poet)

AUGUST

1
The eighth was August, being rich arrayed
The garment all of gold, down to the ground;
Yet rode he not, but led a lovely maid
Forth by the lily hand, the which was crowned
With ears of corn.
Edmund Spenser

2
Here are the cool mosses deep,
And through the moss the ivies creep,
And in the stream the long-leaved flowers weep,
And from the craggy ledge the poppy hangs
in sleep.

Alfred, Lord Tennyson

3
Fairest of months! ripe Summer's Queen
The hey-day of the year
With robes that gleam with sunny sheen,
Sweet August doth appear.

R. Combe Miller

Heather or Ling
(*Calluna vulgaris*)

4 Went to a corn-field to gather Poppies, but a
heavy shower early in the day had
dashed most of the blooms. Found three
different species of Persicaria growing
among the corn, and quantities of Hare-bells
Edith Holden

5 Come, let us stray our gladsome way
And view the charms of Nature,
The rustling corn, the fruited thorn.
And every happy creature.

Robert Burns

6 There is no breeze upon the fern,
No ripple on the lake,
Upon her eyrie nods the erne,
The deer has sought the brake

Sir Walter Scott

7 I see the wild flowers, in their summer morn
Of beauty, feeding on joy's luscious hours,
The gay convolvulus, wreathing round the thorn,
Agape for honey showers

John Clare

8 Low was our pretty Cot; our tallest Rose
Peep'd at the chamber-window. We could hear
At silent noon, and eve, and early morn,
The Sea's faint murmur.

Samuel Taylor Coleridge

AUGUST

9
We drove eight miles through Cumberland
lanes between banks covered with
Harebells. Toadflax, and Hawkweed, crowned
by low hedges waving with the long
streamers of Honeysuckle.
Edith Holden

10
And brushing ankle-deep in flowers,
We heard behind the woodbine veil
The milk that bubbled in the pail,
And buzzings of the honied hours.
Alfred, Lord Tennyson

11
The willows weeping trees, that twinkling hoar,
Glanc'd oft upturn'd along the breezy shore,
Low bending o'er the coloured water, fold
Their moveless boughs and leaves like
                            threads of gold.
William Wordsworth

12
The hills are crumpled plains, the plains parterres,
The trees, round, woolly, ready to be clipped,
And if you seek for any wilderness
You find, at best, a park
Elizabeth Barrett Browning

13
Loveliest of lovely things are they,
On earth that soonest pass away,
The rose that lives its little hour
Is prized beyond the sculptured flower.
William Cullen Bryant

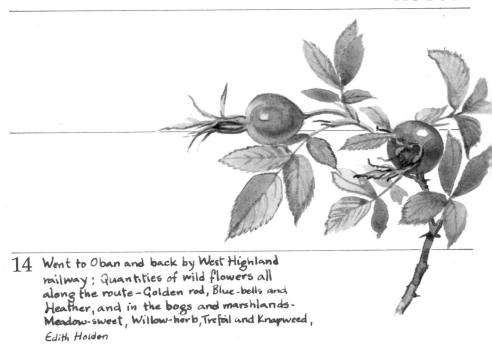

14 Went to Oban and back by West Highland
railway; Quantities of wild flowers all
along the route – Golden rod, Blue-bells and
Heather, and in the bogs and marshlands –
Meadow-sweet, Willow-herb, Trefoil and Knapweed,

Edith Holden

15 An English home: grey twilight pour'd
On dewy pastures, dewy trees,
Softer than sleep – all things in order stored,
A haunt of ancient peace

Alfred, Lord Tennyson

16 There was a time when meadow, grove, and stream;
The earth, and every common sight,
To me did seem
Apparelled in celestial light

William Wordsworth

AUGUST

17 Very bright clear day, with wonderfully fine
distant views. On the high ridge of hills
between Aberfoil and the Trossachs I found
the bright scarlet berries of the Bear-berry
growing among the heather, and Sundew in flower
Edith Holden

18 Wandering by the river's edge,
I love to rustle through the sedge,
And through the woods of reed to tear
Almost as high as bushes are.
John Clare

19 Hail to thee, blithe spirit!
Bird thou never wert,
That from heaven, or near it,
Pourest thy full heart
In profuse strains of unpremeditated art.
To a Skylark, Percy Bysshe Shelley

20 Let the rose glow intense and warm the air,
And let the clouds of even and of morn
Float in voluptuous fleeces o'er the hills;
Let the red wine within the goblet boil,

Hyperion, John Keats

21 It may indeed be phantasy, when I
Essay to draw from all created things
Deep, heartfelt, inward joy that closely clings;
And trace in leaves and flowers that round me lie
Lessons of love and earnest piety.
Samuel Taylor Coleridge

22 And air-swept lindens yield
   Their scent, and rustle down their perfum'd showers
   Of bloom on the bent grass where I am laid,
   And bower me from the August sun with shade.
   Matthew Arnold

23 Found numbers of beautiful little purple
   Heart's-ease growing on the short turf and
   came upon a big bog full of Grass of
   Parnassus, in the midst of the Heather
   and Juniper bushes.
   Edith Holden

AUGUST

---

24   Honey from out the gnarled hive I'll bring,
       And apples wan with sweetness gather thee,-
       Cresses that grow where no man may them see

       John Keats

---

25   The berries on tree and bush are beginning
       to make themselves conspicuous, notably
       the Rowans, Wild Raspberries, which are very
       plentiful in the Highlands, and the hips of a species of
       Wild Rose which has very large crimson fruit.

       Edith Holden

---

26   But pleasures are like poppies spread,
       You seize the flow'r, its bloom is shed;
       Or like the snow falls in the river,
       A moment white — then melts for ever

       Tam o' Shanter, Robert Burns

---

27   Now this sweet vision of my boyish hours
       Free as spring clouds and wild as summer flowers
       Is faded all - a hope that blossomed free
       And hath been once no more shall ever be.

       The Mores, John Clare

---

28   As I was walking across the fields to the
       Cattle today, a Snipe flew up from the grass
       at my feet; soon after I saw a Curlew
       alight in the field, There were numbers of
       Starlings running round about the cattle.

       Edith Holden

29
She lived where the mountains go down to the sea,
And river and tide confer,
Golden Rowan of Menolowan,
Was the name they gave to her.
    Bliss Carman.

30
Beneath yon birch with silver bark,
And boughs so pendulous and fair,
The brook falls scattered down the rock;
And all is mossy there!
    Samuel Taylor Coleridge

31
The calmest thoughts come round us; as of leaves
Budding – fruit ripening in stillness – Autumn suns
Smiling at eve upon the quiet sheaves.
    John Keats

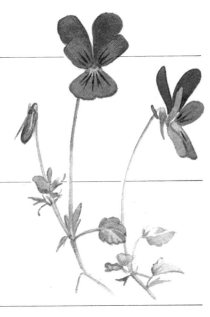

September

Birthdays in September

September 11th	1885	D. H. Lawrence (novelist)
September 13th	1894	J. B. Priestley (writer)
September 18th	1596	James Shirley (dramatist and poet)
	1709	Samuel Johnson (writer)
September 24th	1717	Horace Walpole (writer)
September 29th	1810	Elizabeth Gaskell (writer)

SEPTEMBER

1
Hottest day we have had here yet. This is the
third day of bright sunshine. Cycled through
Doune to Dunblane, through well-wooded,
rolling country, with low hills and fine,
distant views.

Edith Holden

2
Best I love September's yellow,
Morns of dew-strung gossamer;
Thoughtful days without a stir

Alexander Smith

3
Next him September marched eke on foot,
Yet he was hoary, laden with the spoil
Of harvest riches, which he made his boot,
And him enriched with bounty of the soil

Edmund Spenser

4
The splendour falls on castle walls
And snowy summits old in story,
The long light shakes across the lakes;
And the wild cataract leaps in glory.

Alfred, Lord Tennyson

5
O, for a draught of vintage! that hath been
Cool'd a long age in the deep-delved earth,
Tasting of Flora and the country green,
Dance, and Provencal song, and sunburnt mirth!

John Keats

6   All things that love the sun are out of doors;
    The sky rejoices in the morning's birth;
    The grass is bright with rain-drops; - on the moors
    The hare is running races in her mirth

    William Wordsworth

7   September blows soft, -
    Till the fruits in the loft

    Anon

8   Ay me, ay me, I sigh to see the scythe afield:
    Down goeth the grass, soon wrought to withered hay,
    Ay me, alas, ay me, alas, that beauty needs must yield,
    And princes pass, as grass doth fade away!

    Anon

Goldfinch
feeding on
Thistle-seed

9 Winter is cold-hearted,
Spring is yea and nay,
Autumn is a weathercock
Blown every way

Christina Rossetti

10 I bring fresh showers for the thirsting flowers,
From the seas and the streams;
I bear light shade for the leaves when laid
In their noonday dreams.

The Cloud, Percy Bysshe Shelley

11 Behold her, single in the field,
Yon solitary Highland Lass!
Reaping and singing by herself;
Stop here, or gently pass!

William Wordsworth

12 The sun is coming down to earth, and the fields
and the waters shout to him golden shouts.

George Meredith

13 Ceres, most bounteous Lady, thy rich Leas
Of Wheate, Rye, Barley, Vetches, Oates and Pease;
Thy Turphie-Mountaines, where live nibling Sheepe,
And flat Medes thatchd with Stover, them
to keepe

The Tempest, William Shakespeare

SEPTEMBER

14 To one who has been long in city pent,
'Tis very sweet to look into the fair
And open face of heaven, - to breathe a prayer
Full in the smile of the blue firmament.

Escape from the city, John Keats

15 The town was hush'd beneath us: lower down
The bay was oily-calm; the harbour-buoy
With one green sparkle ever and anon
Dipt by itself, and we were glad at heart.

Alfred, Lord Tennyson

16 The wisest, happiest, of our kind are they
That ever walk content with Nature's way,
God's goodness - measuring bounty as it may

William Wordsworth

17 The reflected light on the Eastern hilltops was
gorgeous, - all shades of gold and red and
brown, deepening into purple and grey shadows
at the base of the mountains

Edith Holden

18 Thus harvest ends its busy reign,
And leaves the fields their peace again,
Where autumn's shadows idly muse
And tinge the trees in many hues

John Clare

Horse Chesnut
(Œsculus Hippocastanum)

19 A wind sways the pines,
            And below
Not a breath of wild air;
Still as the mosses that glow
On the flooring
George Meredith

20 Heavily hangs the broad sunflower
Over its grave i' the earth so chilly;
Heavily hangs the hollyhock,
Heavily hangs the tiger-lily.

Alfred, Lord Tennyson

21 Up the airy mountain,
Down the rushy glen,
We daren't go a-hunting
For fear of little men

William Allingham

22 Most of the Chesnut trees were green and
vigorous, with wonderful, twisted trunks
and covered with fruit, as were the Nut trees.
The ruined walls of the Priory were green with
the tiny Wall Spleenwort.
Edith Holden

23 While ripening corn grew thick and deep,
And here and there men stood to reap,
One morn I put my heart to sleep,
And to the meadows took my way.

Jean Ingelow

24 Leaves have their time to fall,
And flowers to wither at the North-wind's breath,
And stars to set; - but all,
Thou hast all seasons for thine own. O Death!

Mrs Felicia Hemans

25 Goodbye to Scotland and back to the
Midlands once more.

Edith Holden

26 My heart's in the Highlands, my heart is not here;
My heart's in the Highlands a chasing the deer;
Chasing the wild deer, and following the roe;
My heart's in the Highlands, wherever I go.

Robert Burns

27 My heart is like a singing bird
Whose nest is in a watered shoot;
My heart is like an apple-tree
Whose boughs are bent with thickset fruit.

Christina Rossetti

28 The stalks and blades,
   Chequer my tablet with their quivering shades,
   On one side is a field of drooping oats,
   Through which the poppies show their scarlet coats

   John Keats

29 Plant trees at Michaelmas and command
                  them to grow
   Set them at Candlemas and entreat
                  them to grow

   Anon

30 Scarcely any of the foliage on the trees
   is turned colour. Some of the Beech trees
   are quite bare, the leaves having
   shrivelled up and fallen off.

   Edith Holden

October

Birthdays in October

October 13th	1797 Thomas Haynes Bayly (dramatist and poet)
October 16th	1854 Oscar Wilde (writer)
October 18th	1784 James Henry Leigh Hunt (writer)
	1785 Thomas Love Peacock (novelist and poet)
October 21st	1687 Edmund Waller (poet)
	1772 Samuel Taylor Coleridge (Poet and writer)
October 25th	1800 Thomas Babington Macaulay (writer)
October 28th	1903 Evelyn Waugh (novelist)
October 29th	1740 James Boswell (writer)
October 30th	1751 Richard Sheridan (dramatist)
October 31st	1795 John Keats (poet)

OCTOBER

1
I brought in some long necklaces of the
bright scarlet berries of the Black Bryony,
and some boughs laden with Chesnuts,
to paint.

Edith Holden

2
Then came October, full of merry glee.

Edmond Spenser

3
... every morning I used to watch the House
Martins from my bed-room window, collecting
in great flocks on the house-roofs, preparatory
to their departure.

Edith Holden

4
Yet the lark's shrill fife may come
At the day-break from the fallow,
And the bittern sounds his drum,
Booming from the sedgy shallow.

Sir Walter Scott

5
Today I was watching a number of Sparrows
and Tom-tits fluttering round, and hanging
on to the heads of the Sunflowers that are
all gone to seed in the garden.

Edith Holden

Fruit
of Dog Rose (*Rosa canina*)
and
Blackberry (

OCTOBER

6 As yet the blue-bells linger on the sod
   That copes the sheepfold ring, and in the woods
   A second blow of many flowers appears,
   Flowers faintly tinged and breathing no perfume.

   James Grahame

7 Here the bleak mount,
   The bare bleak mountain speckled thin with sheep;
   Grey clouds, that shadowing spot the sunny fields;
   And river, now with bushy rocks o'er-browed

   Samuel Taylor Coleridge

8 Season of mists and mellow fruitfulness!
   Close bosom-friend of the maturing sun;
   Conspiring with him how to load and bless
   With fruits the vines that round the
                                          thatch-eaves run
   John Keats

9 Ay, Charles! I knew that this would fix thine eyes
   This woodbine wreathing round the broken porch
   Its leaves just withering, yet one autumn flower
   Still fresh and fragrant

   Robert Southey

10 The hedges are gay with berries of all kinds,—
   Hips and Haws, Elderberries, Bryony,
   Bitter-sweet, Guelder Rose, and Blackberries,
   — and the birds were busy feasting among
   them.
   Edith Holden

11 A last remains of sunset dimly burned
O'er the far forests, – like a torch-flame turned
By the wind back upon its bearer's hand
In one long flare of crimson; as a brand,

Sordello, Robert Browning

12 Now Autumn's fire burns slowly along the woods,
And day by day the dead leaves fall and melt,
And night by night the monitory blast
Wails in the 'key-hole, telling how it pass'd.

William Allingham

13 Yon hanging woods, that touched by autumn seem
As they were blossoming hues of fire and gold;
The flower-like woods, most lovely in decay,
The many clouds, the sea, the rock, the sands,
Lie in the silent moonshine

Samuel Taylor Coleridge

OCTOBER

14 The cottage gardens are very gay just now
with Chrysanthemums, Dahlias, and
Michaelmas Daisies, and the cottage walls
are covered with great splashes of
crimson, where the Virginia creeper has
                                  turned colour.

Edith Holden

15 In October dung your field
And your land it's wealth shall yield.

Anon

16 My sister sent me some lovely crimson
toad-stools with white spots, this
morning, from Keston Common.

Edith Holden

17 How sweet on this autumnal day
The wild-wood fruits to gather,
And on my true-love's forehead plant
A crest of blooming heather!

William Wordsworth

18 O Hesperus! thou bringest all good things —
Home to the weary, to the hungry cheer,
To the young bird the parent's brooding wings,
The welcome stall to the o'erlaboured steer

George Gordon, Lord Byron

19 Or let autumn fall on me
Where a field I linger,
Silencing the bird on tree;
Biting the blue finger.
R.L. Stevenson.

20 Pale the rain-rutted roadways shine
In the green light
Behind the cedar and the pine;
Come thundering night!

George Meredith

21 About a fortnight ago a chiff-chaff was
constantly to be seen hopping about the
goose-berry bushes in the garden:- the
last to leave us, he is usually the first
to arrive.
Edith Holden.

OCTOBER

22 Calm and deep peace, on this high wold;
And on these dews that drench the furze,
And all the silvery gossamers
That twinkle into green and gold.

Alfred, Lord Tennyson

23 I love the fitful gust that shakes
The casement all the day,
And from the mossy elm tree takes
The faded leaves away

John Clare

24 Vast pallid clouds! blue spaces undefiled!
Room! give me room! give loneliness and air!
Free things and plenteous in your regions fair.

George Macdonald

25 I was shown some wonderfully fine
specimens of the Parasol Fungus today,
pale fawn, flecked and shaded with
darker tones of the same colour.

Edith Holden

26 Not a breath of air
Ruffles the bosom of this leafy glen.
From the brook's margin, wide around, the trees
Are steadfast as the rocks

William Wordsworth

27 Under a dark, red-fruited
Yew-tree's shade!
Matthew Arnold

28 Keen fitful gusts are whispering here and there
Among the bushes, half leafless and dry;
The stars look very cold about the sky,
And I have many miles on foot to fare
John Keats

29 The freshness of the heart can fall like dew,
Which out of all the lovely things we see
Extracts emotions beautiful and new;
Hived in our bosoms like the bag o' the bee
George Gordon, Lord Byron

30 Nature now spreads around, in dreary hue,
A pall to cover all that summer knew;
Yet, in the poet's solitary way,
Some pleasing objects for his praise delay
John Clare

31 Mild and damp, with one or two gleams
of sun-shine. The weather throughout
the whole of October, has been very mild.
Edith Holden

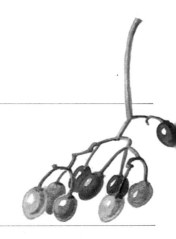

NOVEMBER

Birthdays in November

November 1st	1871	Stephen Crane (writer)
November 3rd	1794	William Cullen Bryant (poet)
November 13th	1850	Robert Louis Stevenson (writer)
November 18th	1836	W.S. Gilbert (writer and librettist)
November 19th	1692	Thomas Shadwell (poet)
November 20th	1752	Thomas Chatterton (poet)
November 22nd	1819	George Eliot (writer)
November 24th	1713	Laurence Sterne (novelist)
November 26th	1731	William Cowper (poet)
November 28th	1628	John Bunyan (writer)
	1757	William Blake (poet and painter)
November 30th	1554	Philip Sidney (poet)
	1667	Jonathan Swift (satirist and poet)

NOVEMBER

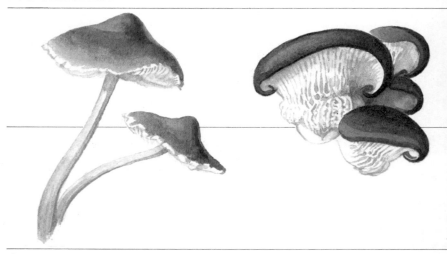

1   Next was November; he full grosse and fat
    As fed with lard, and that right well might seeme;
    For he had been a fatting hogs of late
    That yet his browes with sweat did reek
                    and steem
    Edmund Spenser

2   The year lies dying in this evening light;
    The poet musing in autumnal woods;
    Hears melancholy sighs
    Among the withered leaves.

    from the German

3   I brought home a little book on British Toad-
    stools today, with photographs of 65
    different varieties . I was disappointed not to
    find my beautiful scarlet, spotted toad-stool
    among them.
    Edith Holden

4

November chill blaws loud wi'angry sugh;
The shortening winter-day is near a close;
The miry beasts retreating frae the pleugh;
The blackening trains o'craws to their repose

Robert Burns

6

O if my lips, which are for ever dumb
Could sing to men what my sad heart has heard
Life's darkest hour with songs of joy would ring,
Life's blackest frost would blossom into Spring.

Edmond Holmes

5

When all aloud the wind doth blow,
And coughing drowns the parson's saw,
And bird's sit brooding in the snow,
And Marion's nose looks red and raw.

William Shakespeare

7

The warm sun is failing, the bleak wind is wailing,
The bare boughs are sighing, the pale flowers are dying,
            And the year
On the earth her death-bed, in a shroud of leaves dead,
        Is lying.

Percy Bysshe Shelley

8

O thou whose face hath felt the Winter's wind,
Whose eye has seen the snow-clouds hung in mist,
And the black elm tops 'mong the freezing stars,
To thee the spring will be a harvest-time.

What the Thrush Said, John Keats

9 These early November hours
That crimson the creeper's leaf across
Like a splash of blood, intense, abrupt,
O'er a shield
Robert Browning

10 Went out Fungi-hunting again; I went through
the meadows this time. I came upon the
stumps of two old trees on the bank of a
field, completely covered with masses of a
large flat toad-stool.
Edith Holden

11 November dawns and dewy-glooming downs,
The gentle shower, the smell of dying leaves,
And the low moan of leaden-colour'd seas.
Alfred, Lord Tennyson

12 Yet but awhile the slumbering weather flings
Its murky prison round – then winds wake loud;
With sudden stir the startled forest sings
Winter's returning song – cloud races cloud
John Clare

13 Many of the trees are quite bare, but the
Oaks still have their foliage and were all
shades of bronze and brown, the hedges and
banks too were flowing with the golden
tints of Nut leaves and bracken.
Edith Holden

Green Woodpecker
(Gecinus viridis)

NOVEMBER

14 I saw a kingfisher fly across the little pool
by the roadside below Olton station today.

Edith Holden

15 All the way along, the leaves were whirling
down from the trees in hundreds and
dancing along the road before me.

Edith Holden

16 Fragrant steams from oak-leaves sere,
Peat and moss and whortles green,
Dews that yet are glistening clear
Through their brown or briary screen.

Reverend John Keble

17 Calm and deep peace in this wide air,
These leaves that redden to the fall,
And in my heart, if calm at all,
If any calm, a calm despair

Alfred, Lord Tennyson

18 Come, months, come away,
From November to May,
In your saddest array;
Follow the bier
Of the dead cold year.

Percy Bysshe Shelley

19 That time of yeare thou maist in me behold,
    When yellow leaves, or none, or few doe hange
    Upon those boughes which shake against the could,
    Bare ruin'd quiers, where late the sweet birds sang.
    In me thou seest the twi-light of such day.
    William Shakespeare

20 Sing on sweet thrush, upon the leafless bough,
    Sing on sweet bird. I listen to thy strain,
    And agèd Winter, mid his early reign,
    At thy blythe carol, clears his furrowed brow
    Robert Burns

NOVEMBER

21 'I play for Seasons; not Eternities!'
Says Nature, laughing on her way. 'So must
All those whose stake is nothing more than dust!'
And lo, she wins, and of her harmonies
She is full sure!
George Meredith

22 I love to see the cottage smoke
Curl upwards through the trees,
The pigeons nestled round the cote
On November days like these
John Clare

23 November take flail,
Let no ships sail!
Anon

24 The wind blew as 'twad blawn its last;
The rattling showers rose on the blast;
The speedy gleams the darkness swallowed;
Loud deep, and lang, the thunder bellowed
Robert Burns

25 The mellow year is hastening to its close;
The little birds have almost sung their last,
Their small notes twitter in the dreary blast—
That shrill-piped harbinger of early snows
November, Hartley Coleridge

26 I heard a Thrush singing in the big Beech
tree at the top of Kineton Lane.

Edith Holden

27 O Wild West Wind, thou breath of Autumn's being,
Thou, from whose unseen presence the leaves dead
Are driven like ghosts from an enchanter fleeing,
Yellow and black, and pale, and hectic red

Percy Bysshe Shelley

28 Life said, As thou hast carved me, such am I.
Then memory, like the nightjar on the pine,
And sightless hope, a woodlark in night sky,
Joined notes of Death and Life till night's decline

George Meredith

29 With blackest moss the flower-plots
Were thickly crusted, one and all;
The rusted nails fell from the knots
That held the peach to the garden-wall

Mariana, Alfred, Lord Tennyson

30 O what can ail thee, knight-at-arms,
Alone and palely loitering?
The sedge has withered from the lake,
And no birds sing

Endymion, John Keats

DECEMBER

Birthdays in December

December 4th	1835	Samuel Butler (writer)
December 5th	1830	Christina Rossetti (poet)
December 9th	1608	John Milton (poet)
December 14th	1791	Charles Wolfe (poet)
December 16th	1775	Jane Austen (writer)
December 17th	1873	Ford Madox Ford (writer)
December 24th	1754	George Crabbe (poet)
	1822	Matthew Arnold (poet)
December 25th	1642	Sir Isaac Newton (philosopher)
December 26th	1716	Thomas Gray (poet)
December 30th	1865	Rudyard Kipling (writer)

DECEMBER

1

Today I put out a cocoa-nut to the great
joy of the Tom-tits', numbers of them were
pecking away at it all through the day, -
mostly Blue-tits.

Edith Holden

2

And after him came next the chill December,
Yet he, through merry feasting which he made
And great bon-fires did not the cold remember,
His Saviour's birth his mind so much did glad.

Edmund Spenser

3

      this winter rose
Blossoms amid the snows,
A symbol of God's promise, care and love.

Anon

4

Yet in a little close, however keen
The winter comes, I find a patch of green,
Where robins, by the miser winter made
Domestic, flirt and perch upon the spade

John Clare

5

Yet shall your ragged moor receive
The incomparable pomp of eve,
And the gold glories of the dawn
Behind your shivering trees be drawn

R.L. Stevenson

6   Thanks to the human heart by which we live,
    Thanks to its tenderness, its joys, and fears,
    To me the meanest flower that blows can give
    Thoughts that do often lie too deep for tears.
      William Wordsworth

7   Crowds of birds came to be fed this
    morning. There were great battles among
    the Tits over the cocoa-nut; and once a
    Robin got right into it and refused to
    let the Tits approach
      Edith Holden

8   Sharp is the night, but stars with frost alive
    Leap off the rim of earth across the dome.
    It is a night to make the heavens our home
    More than the nest whereto apace we strive.
      George Meredith

DECEMBER

9 We woke up to a storm of whirling snowflakes
this morning - the first snow this winter.
The storm was soon over however and it
was followed by bright sunshine and
a sharp frost at night.

Edith Holden

10 Cold, frosty day. It seems as if winter
had begun in earnest, but the forecasts
prophecy a speedy change.

Edith Holden

11 In drear-nighted December,
Too happy, happy tree,
Thy Branches ne'er remember
Their green felicity

John Keats

12 Wind and rain with bright intervals.
There was a most beautiful rain-bow
visible in the morning for about ten
minutes.

Edith Holden

13 A widow bird sat mourning for her love
Upon a wintry bough;
The frozen wind crept on above,
The freezing stream below

Winter, Percy Bysshe Shelley

14 Amid the leafless thorn
the merry Wren,
When icicles hand dripping rock;
Apes her perennial lay

James Grahame

15 Old Winter! Seated in thy great armed chair,
Watching the children at their Christmas mirth,
Or circled by them as thy lips declare
Some merry jest, or tale of murder dire

Robert Southey

16 Its verdure trails
the Ivy shoot
Along the ground
from root to root.

Bishop Mant

17 How like a winter hath my absence been
From thee, the pleasure of the fleeting year!
What freezings have I felt, what dark days seen!
What old December's bareness everywhere!

William Shakespeare

18 It was a winter such as when birds die
In the deep forests; and the fishes lie
Stiffened in the translucent ice

Percy Bysshe Shelley

DECEMBER

19 The frost was on the village roofs as white as ocean foam,
The good red fires were burning bright in every
   'long shore home;
The windows sparkled clear, and the chimneys volley'd out;
And I vow we sniff'd the victuals as the vessel went about.
Christmas at Sea , Robert Louis Stevenson

20 After a rapid thaw and four days of
wonderfully mild, still weather, without
wind or rain; the wind has gone round to the
east and it looks as if we might have a
frosty Christmas after all.
Edith Holden

21 Christmas is coming, the geese are getting fat
Please put a penny in the old man's hat
If you haven't got a penny, a ha'penny will do,
If you haven't got a ha'penny, God bless you!

   Beggar's Rhyme

22 Heigh, ho! sing heigh, ho! unto the Green Holly,
Most friendship is feigning, most loving mere folly:
Then, heigh, ho! the holly!
This life is most jolly

   As You Like It, William Shakespeare

23 Bounce buckram velvets dear
Christmas comes but once a year,
When it comes it brings good cheer,
And when its gone, its never near

   Anon

24 Glad Christmas comes, and every hearth
    Makes room to give him welcome now,
    E'en want will dry its tears in mirth,
    And crown him with a holly bough
       Jonn Clare

25 We woke to a snowy Christmas morning;
    sunshine later and sharp frost at night.
       Edith Holden

26 Their wintry garment of unsullied snow
    The mountains have put on.
       Robert Southey

DECEMBER

27 In the paper today it reports that all
Britain lies under snow from John
O'Groats to Land's End for the first
time for six years.

Edith Holden

28 Skating has commenced in the Fens.

Edith Holden

29 And in the frosty season, when the sun
Was set, and visible for many a mile
The cottage windows blazed through twilight gloom,
I heeded not their summons

William Wordsworth

30 I have noticed chaffinches feeding among
the other birds the last few days, they
seldom come to feed; though in the Spring
they are often to be seen on the lawn.

Edith Holden

31 Ring out the old, ring in the new,
Ring, happy bells, across the snow:
The Year is going, let him go;
Ring out the false, ring in the true.

Alfred, Lord Tennyson